RE-ELECT
DONALD J. TRUMP
OUR 45TH PRESIDENT
OF THE
UNITED STATES
OF AMERICA

By Phyllis Finnell

Table of Contents

Introduction

The Office of President of The United States

Our president should always be respected even if we don't agree on the rules and regulations being enforced. The media tends to single him out and give him a hard time promoting "fake news" and other things that no other president of the United States of America has gone through. He has a hard job just trying to run our country and dealing with unruly people.

Many people think that they could do a better job, but I think just one day of dealing with the problems that President Trump has faced would make most people want to give up and quit.

President Trump is a strong and kind man. After all, he did give almost everyone in the United States of America a stimulus check to help them get through hard times. He didn't have to do that, he chose to. President Obama was giving money to many other countries, when they had emergency situations and our current president puts America first.

He always puts America first so on November 2nd, don't make a mistake and vote for the democrats, vote straight for the Republican party.

President Trump Is Doing A Great job of "Making America Great Again." Even in this crisis that America and the WHOLE world is going through. We are a GREAT NATION and blessed to be living in The United States of America. We are BLESSED by GOD.

Inauguration of President Trump

300,000 to 600,000 people attended President Trump's inauguration ceremony on Friday, January 20th, 2017 at the United States Capital in Washington, D.C. President Trump became our 45th president on that day. The event was the 58th presidential inauguration. President Trump had many important people attending his ceremony. Vice President Pence, President Obama, President Clinton and Hillary, Senator Biden, and also Franklin Graham came to his inauguration. There were many other important people there but the people I mentioned were some of the ones that the tv networks happened to allow cameras to focus on.

The presidential inauguration ceremony was very beautiful. As you can see in the picture below, President Trump had many of his friends and family members attending the ceremony that day.

Picture above is of Donald Trump and his wife Melania Trump at the Liberty Ball Inauguration Photo by the U.S. Army/Army Sgt. Ashley Marble. On the Left: President Donald Trump being sworn in on January 20, 2017 at the U.S. Capitol building in Washington, D.C. He holds his left hand on two versions of the Bible, one childhood Bible given to him by his mother, along with Abraham Lincoln's Bible.

Copyright © by The White House

from The Official White House Facebook Page

President Trump's Campaign Promises

Trump signing Executive Order 13769

Protecting the Nation from Foreign Terrorist Entry into the United States (PD-USGOV)

On the first day that President Trump took office, he was working hard to "Make America Great Again." He signed a list of " Executive Orders" to fulfill as many of his "campaign promises" as possible.

President Trump has had many "executive orders" that have passed and also a few that were not passed but in the first 100 days in office, he signed many more bills than any of the other presidents that were before him.

President Trump is proud of The United States of America. He has tried hard to build up our economy, help people in a time of a medical crisis, and also get along with our allies to help build a more peaceful world.

President Trump is proud of The United States of America and takes pride in our country to do his best to make companies prosper, individual Americans prosper, and the United States Of America's people and the whole world, live more healthy and peaceful lives.

Trump signing Executive Order 13780

Sean Spicer, White House Press Secretary

@ twitter / Public domain

President Trump's Family

President Trump is loyal to his family and real estate business. His family owns real estate, they are active in the entertainment business, they own other businesses, and are also involved in politics. President Trump was born on June 14, 1946, in New York and is married to Melania Trump. She was born and named Melanija Knavs in Slovenian and later changed her name to Melania which is American. On January 22, 2005, Melania and Donald Trump were married. Melania is a former model and the third wife of President Trump.

President Trump and Melania have one son and his name is Barron. He just turned 14 years old recently and is handsome just like his dad. President Trump has five children and ten grand-children. His other family members are: Ivana Trump, Marla Maples, Mary Anne MacLeod Trump, Frederick Trump, Elizabeth Christ Trump, John George Trump and Maryanne Trump Barry.

Picture on the right is of Melania Trump.

The Official First Lady Portrait

by Regine Mahaux.

President Trump's Food Choices

This is a short list of foods that are eaten by our president. President Trump likes to eat KFC, mac and cheese, and Oreos. President Trump loves McDonald's. He prefers to eat the fish fillet sandwich or a Big Mac. He was in a McDonald's TV Commercial in 2002. "In 2012, President Trump tweeted that he's never seen a thin person drinking Diet Coke."

Mr. Trump loves his steak "well done." One of his favorite foods is meatloaf. He also loves ketchup to go with his meatloaf and steak. President Trump likes to eat two scoops of ice cream each day with his pie.

Finally, these choices are tasty but please eat broccoli in August to remember good health. We all have to make food choices that are good and many more times they are bad but if we are all honest, we all make unhealthy food choices occasionally. President Trump can eat anything he chooses after all, he is one of the best Presidents that the United States of America has ever had. I have chosen many of these foods myself and love to eat out as often as I can, and that is one of the many things I have missed during the coronavirus situation.

Yes, it is so delicious! Let's share it with everyone.
Melania, would you like some Kentucky Fried Chicken?
KFC
Drawing ©
by Lilly
This picture was given to the author free with love and drawn with love, also it will always be remembered by the author.
Thank you Lillly!

PRESIDENT TRUMP'S
NEW HEALTHIER FOOD CHOICES

On March 3rd, 2018, President Trump decided to change his diet to a more healthier diet. He is eating more soup and salad now. Here are a few of my recipes that I would like to send to President Trump. He might need to make the recipes larger if anyone else would be eating besides his wife because most of my recipes are only smaller portions for small families. My recipes are healthy just like Dr. Joel Furhman's recipes. He is an excellent doctor. He has a book on www.amazon.com called, *Eat To Live*.

This is only 3 of my recipes.

1. Esau's Red Lentil Stew

Ingredients:

1. Red Lentils------- 1 cup

2. 1/2 tsp. salt

3. 2 cups hot water

Cooking Instructions:

Rinse your lentils before cooking. Place in a small pot after rinsing and add warm water and salt.

Place on the stove on high for 5 minutes. Then, turn your stove down to medium and cook 10 more minutes.

This is like the red lentil stew that Esau sold his birthright to his brother Jacob for, that's mentioned in the Holy Bible in the book of Genesis, Chapter 25: 29-34. Esau gave up his birthright for a bowl of this type soup so you know it has to be excellent. When you cook this soup it smells so good that the whole house smells good! It is delicious.

2. Phyllis's Vegetable Soup

Ingredient list:

(Use all organic ingredients, if possible.)

1. 1 large onion

2. 2 garlic cloves

3. 4 large carrots

4. 1 ear corn on cob

5. 6 stalks celery

6. 1/2 cup red lentils

7. 1 cup brown organic rice

8. 64 oz. 100 percent vegetable juice (clover valley made in U. S.A.)

9. 3 tsps. oregano

10. 3 tsp parsley

11. 1 pint filtered water

12. Salt (to your preference). I used 1 tbsp.

This is not salty if you're watching your salt.

Cooking Instructions:

Use all organic vegetables, if possible.

Cut up your onion and garlic in a large bowl. Next, slice 4 large carrots. Then, cut your corn off of the cob and scrape the cob to get the pulp out.

Chop your celery into bite sizes. Pour all these vegetables into a large pot. Rinse your red lentils and add to the pot. Then, add brown rice. Next, add the 64oz. container of 100 percent vegetable juice to the pot. Add your parsley and oregano, stir your spices up. Add filtered water and salt. Finally, wash 3 white potatoes and cut them up. Then, add to the pot. Place lid on the pot and cook on high for 15 minutes; then, turn down the stove to medium for the last 15 minutes. After stove is off, let the pot set on the eye for another 15 minutes; then, serve.

3. PHYLLIS'S CLEVELAND, TENNESSEE or BRADLEY COUNTY / COSTA RICA SALAD

All ingredients should come from Cleveland, Tennessee or the Bradley county area and be organic except the pineapple.

1. Kale And Lettuce (1 bunch each)

2. Celebrity Tomatoes (3)

3. 2 Slices of Fresh Costa Rica Pineapple

Cut up all ingredients and put in a large bowl, toss. Serve in salad bowls. Serve with your favorite salad dressing.

North Korea's Leader Kim Jong-Un

President Trump shakes the hand of Kim Jong-Un at the Singapore Summit on June 12, 2018. A nuclear deal made with Kim Jong-Un and President Trump is called the Korean Peninsula Deal. President Trump is the first president to shake the hand of a North Korean's head of state.

Photo © by Shealah Craighead (PD-US.Gov.)

The July 16, 2018 Trump-Putin Summit

The Russia-United States Summit was a summit meeting between United States President Donald Trump and Russian President Vladimir Putin. (Also known as the Trump-Putin Summit on July 16, 2018 in Helsinki, Finland).

Photo © by Kremlin.ru / CC BY

(https://creativecommons.org/licenses/by/4.0)

Donald Trump's Accomplishments

IGNITING A HISTORIC ECONOMIC BOOM: President Trump's pro-growth policies are unleashing economic growth and providing opportunities to workers across the country.

- Due to President Trump's pro-growth policies, real gross domestic product (GDP) growth exceeded 3 percent over the last four quarters.

- Real GDP grew at annual rates of 3.4 percent in the third quarter of 2018 and 4.2 percent in the second quarter.

- More than 5 million jobs have been created since President Trump's election and the unemployment rate remains below 4 percent.

- This is the eighth time this year that the unemployment rate has been below 4 percent.

- Prior to this year, the unemployment rate had fallen below 4 percent only five times since 1970.

- The unemployment rate for African-Americans in May fell to 5.9 percent, which is the lowest rate on record.

- Asian and Hispanic-American unemployment rates have reached record lows this year.

- Initial weekly jobless claims have hit a nearly 50-year low under President Trump.

- Under President Trump, job openings outnumber the unemployed for the first time on record.

- Recently, more than two-thirds of Americans rated "now" as a good time to find a quality job, tying a record high in a poll by Gallup.

- Americans are seeing more money in their pockets thanks to the booming economy.

- In recent months, workers have seen their largest nominal year over year wage growth in nearly a decade.

- In 2017, real median household income rose to a post-recession high.

- President Trump's policies are helping to lift Americans out of poverty.

- African-American and Hispanic-American poverty rates reached record lows of 21.2 percent and 18.3 percent, respectively, in 2017.

- Since the election, 4.6 million Americans have been lifted off of food stamps.

- Consumer confidence has soared under President Trump, recently reaching an 18-year high.

- President Trump is delivering on his promise to bring back American manufacturing.

- The National Association of Manufacturers' Outlook Index had the highest annual average in its history over the past year.

- Manufacturing added 284,000 jobs in 2018, the most added in a year since 1997.

- Small Business optimism jumped to a record high under President Trump, according to a survey by the National Federation of Independent Business (NFIB).

- The NFIB's Small Business Optimism Index broke a 35-year record in August.

- President Trump signed the Tax Cuts and Jobs Act into law, ushering in the largest package of tax cuts and reforms in American history.

- These tax cuts are delivering real results for American families and workers.

- More than 6 million workers received tax cut bonuses and benefits.

- More than 100 utility companies have announced lower rates.

- President Trump is ensuring American workers receive the training and education they need to compete in today's economy.

- President Trump signed an executive order establishing the National Council for the American worker.

- More than 185 companies and associations have signed our "Pledge to America's Workers," promising more than 6.4 million new training and career opportunities.

- The President signed legislation that reauthorized the Carl D. Perkins Career and Technical Education Act, making more than $1 billion available for career education programs.

- President Trump has prioritized the economic empowerment of women.

- The women's unemployment rate recently reached its lowest rate in 65 years.

- The Small Business Administration lent approximately $500 million more in capital to women-owned businesses in 2017 compared to 2016.

- The Administration helped launch the Women Entrepreneurs Finance Initiative, which could leverage more than $1 billion to support women entrepreneurs.

- Biggest tax cuts and reforms in American history by signing the Tax Cuts and Jobs act into law

- Provided more than $5.5 trillion in gross tax cuts, nearly 60 percent of which will go to families.

- Increased the exemption for the death tax to help save Family Farms & Small Business.

- Nearly doubled the standard deduction for individuals and families.

- Enabled vast majority of American families will be able to file their taxes on a single page by claiming the standard deduction.

- Doubled the child tax credit to help lessen the financial burden of raising a family.

- Lowered America's corporate tax rate from the highest in the developed world to allow American businesses to compete and win.

- Small businesses can now deduct 20 percent of their business income.

- Cut dozens of special interest tax breaks and closed loopholes for the wealthy.

- 9 in 10 American workers are expected see an increase in their paychecks thanks to the tax cuts, according to the Treasury Department.

- More than 6 million of American workers have received wage increases, bonuses, and increased benefits thanks to tax cuts.

- Over 100 utility companies have lowered electric, gas, or water rates thanks to the Tax Cuts and Jobs Act.

- Ernst & Young found 89 percent of companies planned to increase worker compensation thanks to the Trump tax cuts.

- Established opportunity zones to spur investment in left behind communities.

ROLLING BACK RED TAPE: President Trump is rolling back costly regulations that have burdened hardworking Americans and stifled innovation.

- President Trump has followed through on and exceeded his promise to roll back two regulations for every new one created.

- President Trump's Administration surpassed the 2:1 ratio in 2018, eliminating 12 regulations for every new one in 2018.

- In 2017, the Trump Administration eliminated 22 regulations for every new one.

- Since taking office, President Trump's deregulation efforts have achieved $33 billion in regulatory savings.

- In 2018, these efforts alone delivered $23 billion in benefits to American families and business owners.

- President Trump has signed 16 Congressional Review Act resolutions into law, eliminating burdensome Obama-era rules and regulations.

- President Trump announced U.S. withdrawal from the Paris Climate Agreement, which would have harmed America's economy and cost American workers millions of jobs.

- President Trump signed an executive order to streamline the permitting process forinfrastructure projects with a goal of cutting approval time from up to 10 years to an average of 2 years.

- President Trump signed legislation to roll back burdensome Dodd-Frank regulations that harmed community banks.

NEGOTIATING BETTER DEALS FOR THE AMERICAN PEOPLE: President Trump is negotiating fair and balanced trade deals that protect American industries and workers.

- President Trump negotiated a new trade agreement between the United States, Canada, and Mexico to replace the disastrous and outdated North American Free Trade Agreement.

- Once enacted by Congress, the United States–Mexico–Canada Agreement (USMCA) will better serve the interests of American workers and businesses.

- USMCA will incentivize billions of dollars in auto and auto parts production in the United States and create a freer and fairer market for American agriculture.

- USMCA also includes the strongest-ever provisions on labor, environmental, digital, and intellectual property protections to reflect the realities of the 21st century economy.

- The President renegotiated the United States–Korea Free Trade Agreement to preserve and grow jobs in the American auto industry and increase American exports.

- The United States and Japan are set to begin negotiations on a United States–Japan Trade Agreement.

- President Trump is establishing a new trade relationship with the European Union (EU), working toward the elimination of tariff and non-tariff barriers to transatlantic trade.

- President Trump has established a Trade and Investment Working Group to lay the groundwork for post-Brexit trade with the United Kingdom (UK) and has notified Congress of his intent to negotiate a free trade agreement with the UK.

- This year, President Trump filed a withdrawal notification with the Universal Postal Union, launching a one-year negotiation to secure fair international postal rates for American mailers.

- President Trump has expanded market access for American agricultural producers.

- Argentina has opened to American pork and beef, Brazil to American beef, Japan to lamb and Idaho chipping potatoes, South Korea to American poultry, and more.

- The Administration authorized $12 billion to aid farmers affected by unfair retaliatory tariffs.

- The Trump Administration has begun the process to expand the sale of E15, or gasoline containing 15 percent ethanol, to year round.

- Under President Trump, the United States will no longer accept bad trade deals and unfair trade practices that harm American workers and industries.

- One of the President's first actions after taking office was withdrawing the United States from the terrible Trans-Pacific Partnership, which incentivized outsourcing.

- In 2017, the Administration oversaw 82 antidumping and countervailing duty investigations.

- President Trump is holding China accountable for its unfair trade practices, such as the theft of intellectual property, by imposing tariffs on $250 billion in Chinese goods.

- Following President Trump's successful meeting with President Xi in Buenos Aires, both agreed to conduct negotiations over 90 days to address the United States concerns.

- American steel and aluminum jobs are coming back following President Trump's tariffs to protect domestic industries that are vital to national security.

- President Trump imposed tariffs to protect American-made washing machines and solar products that were hurt by import surges.

UNLEASHING AMERICAN ENERGY: President Trump is rolling back costly and burdensome regulations to unleash America's incredible energy resources.

- After years of stifling regulation under the last Administration, President Trump is unleashing America's energy potential.

- America is the largest crude oil producer in the world and production has hit a record high.

- President Trump's policies are helping to boost American energy exports.

- The Administration has streamlined Liquefied Natural Gas terminal permitting.

- In 2017, the United States became a net natural gas exporter for the first time in 60 years.

- American coal exports increased by more than 60 percent in 2017.President Trump is expanding access to our country's abundant natural resources.

- The President signed legislation to open up energy exploration in the Alaska National Wildlife Refuge.

- In July 2018, the Department of the Interior announced it would hold the largest oil and gas lease sale in history.

- In 2017, the Administration approved construction of the Dakota Access pipeline and the cross border permit for the Keystone XL pipeline.

- The Administration issued permits for the New Burgos Pipeline that will export American petroleum products to Mexico.

- The President has ended the war on coal, cutting Obama-era regulations such as the "Stream Protection Rule" which was estimated to cost industries $81 million a year.

- President Trump is replacing the Clean Power Plan, a flawed Obama-era regulation that the Supreme Court ordered halted.

- President Trump rescinded the hydraulic fracturing rule, which was expected to cost the oil and gas industry $32 million per year.

- The Trump Administration curbed the burdensome Obama-era rule on methane, saving American energy developers hundreds of millions of dollars in regulatory costs.

EXPANDING OPTIONS FOR QUALITY AND AFFORDABLE HEALTHCARE: President Trump is expanding access to affordable healthcare choices and taking action to lower drug prices.

- President Trump's Administration is working to provide Americans with affordable alternatives to Obamacare.

- The Administration expanded short-term, limited duration health insurance plans that are expected to be nearly 50 percent cheaper than unsubsidized Obamacare plans.

- President Trump has expanded association health plans, allowing more employers to join together across State lines and affordably offer coverage to their employees.

- The Administration proposed a reform to Health Reimbursement Account (HRA) regulations that will give consumers more freedom to purchase benefits that fit their needs.

- Roughly 800,000 employers are expected to provide HRAs for more than 10 million employees once the rule finalized.

- Americans have more healthcare freedom thanks to the President signing legislation that ended Obamacare's individual mandate penalty.

- While healthcare premiums had been steadily increasing as a result of Obamacare, the average benchmark exchange premium will decline for the first time in 2019 thanks to President Trump's policies.

- Next year, Americans will benefit from more insurer participation on the exchanges.

- Medicare Advantage plans offer more benefit options than ever before, and average premiums in 2019 will be 6 percent lower than in 2018.

- President Trump launched an unprecedented campaign to drive down drug prices, leading more than a dozen drug manufactures to enact price freezes, reductions, or rollbacks.

- In 2018, the Food and Drug Administration (FDA) approved a record number of generic drugs, breaking the previous record set by the Administration in 2017.

- The FDA's Fiscal Year (FY) 2017 generic drug approvals are expected to bring nearly $9 billion in savings in 2017 alone.

- President Trump signed legislation eliminating contractual gag clauses that stopped pharmacists from informing patients about lower drug prices.

- The President put forth an initiative to stop global freeloading that drives up prices for American patients.

- The Administration provided Medicare Advantage and Medicare Part D plans with new negotiating tools to drive down drug costs for American patients.

- The Administration implemented reforms to the amount Medicare pays hospitals for drugs that are purchased under the 340B program, saving seniors $320 million in 2018.

- President Trump signed "Right to Try" legislation to expand access to experimental treatments for terminally ill patients.

FIGHTING BACK AGAINST THE CRISIS NEXT DOOR: President Trump mobilized his entire Administration to combat the opioid crisis that has devastated communities across the country.

- President Trump launched an Initiative to Stop Opioid Abuse and Reduce Drug Supply and Demand, introducing new measures to confront the driving forces behind this crisis.

- The President signed the landmark SUPPORT for Patients and Communities Act, the largest and most comprehensive legislative package addressing a single drug crisis in history.

- The President helped secure a record $6 billion in funding to fight the opioid epidemic.

- The Administration provided more than $2 billion in grants in 2018 to help States, territories, tribes, and local communities prevent and treat opioid abuse.

- The Administration pursued scientific solutions to prevent and treat addiction through the Helping to End Addiction Long-term (HEAL) Initiative.

- The President launched a national public awareness campaign about the dangers of opioid addiction and youth opioid usage.

- Last year, President Trump created a Commission on Combating Drug Addiction and the Opioid Crisis, which recommends ways to tackle the opioid crisis.

- The Administration declared the opioid crisis a nationwide Public Health Emergency in 2017.

- President Trump is working to cut off the flow of deadly opioids into our country and to disrupt the networks that distribute them to our communities.

- The Administration secured first-ever indictments against Chinese nationals for fentanyl trafficking.

- The Department of Justice (DOJ) launched a surge to target fentanyl and heroin dealers in the districts with the most severe overdose death rates.

- The DOJ formed a Joint Criminal Opioid Darknet Enforcement team and shut down the biggest Darknet distributor of drugs.

- Last year, the DOJ announced the largest healthcare fraud takedown in history, arresting more than 120 defendants with opioid-related crimes.

- The President launched a Safer Prescribing Plan that seeks to cut nationwide opioid prescription fills by one-third within three years.

- The Administration has led four National Prescription Drug Take-Back Days, collecting a record-breaking 1,837 tons of expired and unneeded prescription drugs.

STANDING UP FOR THE SANCTITY OF LIFE AND PROTECTING RELIGIOUS LIBERTY: The President is committed to defending the right to life and religious liberty.

- President Trump is the first president to address the March for Life live.

- Shortly after taking office, President Trump reinstated and expanded the Mexico City Policy, blocking $9 billion in aid from funding abortion internationally.

- President Trump defunded a United Nations (UN) agency for colluding with China's brutal program of forced abortion and sterilization.

- The Administration withdrew guidance that constrained State's ability to exclude family-planning providers that provide abortion services from the Medicaid program.

- The Administration formed a new Conscience and Religious Freedom Division to protect religious freedom.

- Expressed strong support for the Pain-Capable Unborn Child Protection Act, which would stop abortions after 20 weeks.

- The Trump Administration proposed new regulations to ensure Title X family planning funding does not go to projects that perform, support, or refer patients for abortion.

- The Trump Administration issued regulations establishing new or expanded exemptions from the Obamacare contraceptive mandate based on religious beliefs or moral convictions.

- In 2017, the President issued an executive order to promote free speech and religious liberty. This helped faith-based groups give healthcare coverage to 13.7 million Americans.

KEEPING AMERICAN COMMUNITIES SAFE: President Trump has made clear that his first responsibility is to protect the safety and security of Americans.

- Federal Bureau of Investigation data shows violent crime decreased under President Trump's watch in 2017, following two consecutive years of increases.

- United States Attorneys indicted the most violent criminals on record last year.

- Last year, the DOJ announced nearly $100 million in grant funding to hire hundreds of additional law enforcement officers.

- President Trump is cracking down on the vile MS-13 gang that has brought violence to communities across the country.

- In 2017, the DOJ worked with international partners to arrest and charge approximately 4,000 MS-13 members.

- Immigration and Customs Enforcement's (ICE) Homeland Security Investigations arrested nearly 800 MS-13 members and associates in FY 2017, an 83 percent increase from the prior year.

- President Trump signed an executive order to restore State and local law enforcement's access to surplus equipment that can be used to help keep our communities safe.

- President Trump enhanced and updated the Project Safe Neighborhoods program.

- The DOJ announced the creation of the National Public Safety Partnership in 2017, launching a cooperative initiative with cities to reduce violent crime.

- President Trump signed legislation to improve the Federal firearm background check system and keep guns out of the hands of dangerous criminals.

- President Trump signed the First Step Act, which includes bipartisan reforms to make our Federal justice system fairer and our communities safer.

- The First Step Act will help prepare inmates to successfully rejoin society, reducing recidivism and improving community safety.

- This legislation includes commonsense sentencing reforms that will make our Federal justice system fairer while keeping violent criminals and sex offenders off our streets.

- Trump's Department of Health and Human Services issued a rule to align grant regulations with current nondiscrimination laws. The announcement stresses that "the federal government [should] not infringe on religious freedom in its operation of HHS grant programs and [seeks to] address the impact of regulatory actions on small entities." The move reverses an Obama-era rule and allow religious adoption agencies that turn away gay couples to receive federal funding. The goal of the new rule is to directly aid faith-based adoption agencies, which often receive federal grants and have been defending themselves against accusations of discrimination.

PROTECTING THE INNOCENT: President Donald J. Trump is taking a stand against human trafficking, dedicating our Government's full resources towards fighting this repulsive crime.

- The President signed the Trafficking Victims Protection Reauthorization Act (S. 1862) which tightens criteria for whether countries are meeting standards for eliminating trafficking.

- He signed the Allow States and Victims to Fight Online Sex Trafficking Act (H.R. 1865), overnight this shut down the most common websites used to sell and abuse victims in America.

- President Trump signed the Frederick Douglass Trafficking Victims Prevention and Protection Reauthorization Act, authorizing $430 million to fight sex and labor trafficking.

- He also signed the Abolish Human Trafficking Act, which strengthens programs supporting survivors and resources for combating modern slavery.

- The President signed the Trafficking Victims Protection Act (S. 1312), establishing new prevention, prosecution, and collaboration initiatives to bring human traffickers to justice.

- In September 2017, Ivanka Trump and Deputy Secretary of State Sullivan joined more than 20 world leaders at the United Nations General Assembly for a global call to end modern slavery and to announce the State Department's $25 million grant to the Global Fund to End Modern Slavery.

- In February 2017, the President signed Executive Order 13773, "Enforcing Federal Law with Respect to Transnational Criminal Organizations and Preventing International Trafficking," which directed the United States government to identify, interdict, disrupt, and dismantle the transnational criminal organizations that engage in human trafficking.

ENFORCING OUR LAWS AND SECURING OUR BORDERS: From the first day of his Administration, President Trump has worked to uphold the rule of law and secure our borders.

- President Trump released an immigration framework that would fix our broken immigration system through merit-based reform and provide the resources needed to secure our border.

- This includes closing the legal loopholes that enable illegal immigration, ending chain migration, and eliminating the visa lottery.

- President Trump secured funding to begin building the wall and construction has already begun in areas along the southern border.

- President Trump deployed the military to assist in securing the southern border.

- President Trump and his Administration took action to require aliens seeking asylum to go to a port of entry to make their claim.

- Customs and Border Protection (CBP) apprehended 17,256 criminals and 1,019 gang members in FY 2018.

- ICE's Enforcement and Removal Operations (ERO) arrested 158,581 aliens in FY 2018, an 11 percent increase from FY 2017.

- 90 percent of those arrested had criminal convictions, pending charges, or had been issued final orders of removal.

- ICE ERO increased removals by 13 percent in FY 2018 to 256,086, the majority of whom were convicted criminals.

- Removals of convicted criminal aliens increased by 14 percent from FY 2017.

- Nearly 6,000 known or suspected gang members were removed in FY 2018, a 9 percent increase from FY 2017.

- The Department of Justice prosecuted a record number of criminal immigration offenses in FY 2018, and increased the number of prosecutions for illegal entry by 84 percent over FY 2017.

- Immigration courts are now completing more cases than at any point since 2011.

- President Trump kept his promise by launching the office of Victims of Immigration Crime Engagement (VOICE) within the Department of Homeland Security.

- The Administration has more than doubled the number of jurisdictions participating in the 287(g) program, which enables State and local law enforcement to aid immigration enforcement.

- President Trump has made our country safer by ordering the enhanced vetting of individuals entering from countries that do not meet our security standards.

- These procedures were upheld in a June 2018 Supreme Court ruling.

REBUILDING AMERICA'S MILITARY FORCE: President Trump is rebuilding our military and defending America's interests across the world.

- President Trump ended the devastating defense cuts of the past Administration and has secured historic investments to rebuild our military.

- President Trump signed legislation providing $700 billion for defense in FY 2018 and $716 billion in FY 2019.

- President Trump is supporting America's men and women in uniform, securing the largest military pay raise in nearly a decade.

- The President issued a new National Security Strategy to keep America safe from all threats.

- The Administration has also released new strategies specific to cybersecurity, biodefense, counterterrorism, and weapons of mass destruction terrorism.

- President Trump directed the first whole-of-government assessment of United States manufacturing and defense supply chains since the Eisenhower Administration.

- President Trump initiated the 2018 Nuclear Posture Review, improving United States deterrence policy and existing capabilities to counter nuclear threats.

- President Trump empowered our military commanders with broad authority in order to take the fight to ISIS, and the results are clear.

- ISIS has lost nearly all of its territory, more than half of which has been liberated since President Trump took office.

- All of ISIS' territory in Iraq was successfully liberated.

- ISIS' self-proclaimed capital city Raqqah has been recaptured.

- ISIS' territorial caliphate has been defeated and President Trump has announced that he is bringing America's troops in Syria home.

- President Trump announced a new Iran strategy to confront all of Iran's malign activities and withdrew from the horrible, one-sided Iran nuclear deal.

- All sanctions that had been lifted or waived under the Iran deal have been reimposed.

- The Administration has sanctioned more than 160 individuals tied to the regime's support of terrorism, ballistic missile program, human rights abuses, and more.

- President Trump took decisive military action to respond to the barbaric use of chemical weapons by the Assad regime.

- President Trump directed strikes in response to the regime's chemical weapons attacks in April 2017 and April 2018.

- The Trump Administration has also rolled out sanctions targeting those tied to Syria's chemical weapons program.

- President Trump is strengthening America's cyber defense and directed the elevation of the United States Cyber Command into a major warfighting command.

- The President announced that the Department of Defense will work to create a Space Force to serve as an independent branch of the United States military.

RESTORING AMERICAN LEADERSHIP ABROAD: President Trump is restoring American leadership on the world stage and advancing an America first agenda.

- President Trump held an historic summit with Chairman Kim Jong-Un, bringing beginnings of peace and denuclearization to the Korean Peninsula.

- Since the summit, the leaders have exchanged letters and high-level officials from both countries have met.

- Because of the President's actions, North Korea has halted nuclear and missile tests.

- The remains of POW/MIA service members from the Korean War are being returned to the United States.

- Prior to the summit, President Trump's leadership helped secure the passage of historic UN sanctions on North Korea.

- President Trump followed through on his promise to recognize Jerusalem as the capital of Israel and move the American embassy there.

- President Trump withdrew the United States from the UN Human Rights Council due to its bias against Israel.

- The Administration made clear that it does not accept the International Criminal Court's jurisdiction over Americans and will continue to protect America's sovereignty.

- President Trump has successfully advocated for cutting waste at the UN.

- Changes made to the organization's structure allowed the UN to cut hundreds of millions of dollars from their budget, while making the organization more efficient.

- The President's leadership in the North Atlantic Treaty Organization (NATO) has encouraged members to increase their defense spending and realign the Alliance's priorities.

- In 2017 alone, there was an increase of more than 4.8 percent in defense spending among NATO allies.

- President Trump convinced the Alliance to strengthen counterterrorism activities, and NATO formally joined the coalition to defeat ISIS.

- President Trump's Administration is working to advance a free and open Indo-Pacific through investments and partnerships.

- President Trump has imposed tough sanctions on the corrupt regimes in Venezuela, Cuba, and Nicaragua.

- President Trump has taken tough action to combat Russia's malign activities, including Russia's efforts to undermine United States elections.

- The Administration has imposed sanctions on more than 200 individuals and entities related to Russia's destabilizing activities.

- The Trump Administration has enhanced support for Ukraine's defense by stepping up sales of weapons to its military.

- The Trump Administration has secured the release of numerous American citizens held abroad, including Pastor Andrew Brunson from Turkey, Josh Holt from Venezuela, and more.

- President Trump attended G20 summits in Argentina and Germany, where he promoted American First policies and encouraged closer cooperation.

- In 2017, President Trump conducted tours through Asia to promote America's interests.

HONORING AMERICA'S COMMITMENT TO OUR VETERANS: President Trump is honoring America's commitment to our veterans by ensuring they receive the quality care they have earned.

- President Trump secured a record $73.1 billion in funding for the Department of Veterans Affairs (VA) to provide quality medical care for our veterans.

- This funding included $8.6 billion for mental health services, $400 million for opioid abuse prevention, $206 million for suicide prevention, and more.

- The President signed the VA MISSION Act, revolutionizing that VA healthcare system and reforming numerous services for our veterans.

- This legislation will consolidate and reform existing programs to give eligible veterans better access to healthcare providers in their communities.

- Thanks to this legislation, eligible veterans will have access to walk-in community clinics that offer immediate, local care.

- President Trump and his Administration have expanded access to telehealth services for veterans, including through the "Anywhere to Anywhere" VA health care initiative.

- President Trump issued an executive order requiring the Administration to improve access to mental health treatment and suicide prevention resources for veterans.

- President Trump signed the Veterans Affairs Accountability and Whistleblower Protection Act, making it easier to fire failing employees and protect whistleblowers.

- Under President Trump, the VA has removed, demoted, or suspended more than 4,300 employees for poor performance.

- President Trump signed the Veterans Appeals Improvement and Modernization Act of 2017, streamlining the process used by veterans when appealing benefits claims.

- President Trump fulfilled his promise to create a new White House VA Hotline to provide veterans with 24/7 support.

- The VA is providing veterans with online access to wait time and quality of care data.

- The President signed the Forever GI Bill, providing veterans, service members, and their families with enhanced education benefits.

- Last year, programs at the VA and the Department of Housing and Urban Development helped more than 51,000 veterans find permanent housing and access supportive services.

TRANSFORMING GOVERNMENT: President Trump has followed through on his pledge to transform the Federal Government and increase accountability and transparency.

- President Trump's Administration submitted a plan to reorganize the executive branch in order to improve efficiency and effectiveness.

- In a historic show of transparency and accountability, the Trump Administration completed the Department of Defense's first ever audit.

- The President implemented a five-year ban on lobbying for White House employees and a lifetime ban on lobbying for foreign countries.

- Each quarter since taking office, President Trump has donated his salary, fulfilling a promise he made to the American people.

- As of December 1, 2019, President Donald Trump had made 164 Article III judicial appointments—2 supreme court justices, 48 appellate court judges, 112 district court judges, and 2 judges on the Court of International Trade.

°List provided by permission of Liberty Counsel

List of The United States Presidents And Their Vice Presidents

1. President:

George Washington (1789–1797)

Unaffiliated

Vice President: John Adams

2. President:

John Adams (1797–1801)

Federalist

Vice President: Thomas Jefferson

3. President:

Thomas Jefferson (1801–1809)

Democratic-
Republican

Vice President: Aaron Burr

George Clinton

4. President:

James Madison (1809–1817)

Democratic-

Republican

Vice President: George Clinton

Elbridge Gerry

5. President:

James Monroe (1817–1825)

Democratic-

Republican

Vice President: Daniel D. Tompkins

6. President:

John Quincy Adams (1825–1829)

Democratic-

Republican

Vice President: John C. Calhoun

7. President:

Andrew Jackson (1829–1837)

Democratic

Vice President: John C. Calhoun

Martin Van Buren

8. President:

Martin Van Buren (1837–1841)

Democratic

Vice President: Richard Mentor Johnson

9. President:

William Henry Harrison (1841)

Whig

Vice President: John Tyler

10. President:

John Tyler (1841–1845)

Whig

Vice President: Vacant through Presidency

11. President:

James K. Polk (1845–1849)

Democratic

Vice President: George M. Dallas

12. President:

Zachary Taylor (1849–1850)

Whig

Vice President: Millard Fillmore

13. President:

Millard Fillmore (1850–1853)

Whig

Vice President: Vacant through Presidency

14. President:

Franklin Pierce (1853–1857)

Democratic

Vice President: William R. King

15. President:

James Buchanan (1857–1861)

Democratic

Vice President: John C. Breckinridge

16. President:

Abraham Lincoln (1861–1865)

Republican

Natural Union

Vice President: Hannibal Hamlin

Andrew Johnson

17. President:

Andrew Johnson (1865–1869)

Natural
Union

Vice President: Vacant through presidency

18. President:

Ulysses S. Grant (1869–1877)

Republican

Vice President: Schuyler Colfax

Henry Wilson

19. President:

Rutherford B. Hayes (1877–1881)

Republican

Vice President: William A. Wheeler

20. President:

James A. Garfield (1881)

Republican

Vice President: Chester A. Arthur

21. President:

Chester A. Arthur (1881–1885)

Republican

Vice President: Vacant through Presidency

22. President:

Grover Cleveland (1885–1889)

Democratic

Served as the
24th
President

Vice President: Thomas A. Hendricks

23. President:

Benjamin Harrison (1889–1893)

Republican

Vice President: Levi P. Morton

24. President:

Grover Cleveland (1893–1897)

Democratic

Served as the

22nd

President

Vice President: Adlai Stevenson I

25. President:

William McKinley (1897–1901)

Republican

Vice President: Garret Hobart

Theodore Roosevelt

26. President:

Theodore Roosevelt (1901–1909)

Republican

Vice President: Charles W. Fairbanks

27. President:

William Howard Taft (1909–1913)

Republican

Vice President: James S. Sherman

28. President:

Woodrow Wilson (1913–1921)

Democratic

Vice President: Thomas R. Marshall

29. President:

Warren G. Harding (1921–1923)

Republican

Vice President: Calvin Coolidge

30. President:

Calvin Coolidge (1923–1929)

Republican

Vice President: Charles G. Dawe

31. President:

Herbert Hoover (1929–1933)

Republican

Vice President: Charles Curtis

32. President:

Franklin D. Roosevelt (1933–1945)

Democratic

Vice President: John Nance Garner

Henry A. Wallace

Harry S. Truman

33. President:

Harry S Truman (1945–1953)

Democratic

Vice President: Alben W. Barkley

34. President:

Dwight D. Eisenhower (1953–1961)

Republican

Vice President: Richard Nixon

35. President:

John F. Kennedy (1961–1963)

Democratic

Vice President: Lyndon B. Johnson

36. President:

Lyndon B. Johnson (1963–1969)

Democratic

Vice President: Hubert Humphrey

37. President:

Richard Nixon (1969–1974)

Republican

Vice President: Spiro Agnew

Gerald Ford

38. President:

Gerald Ford (1974–1977)

Republican

Vice President: Nelson Rockefeller

39. President:

Jimmy Carter (1977–1981)

Democratic

Vice President: Walter Mondale

40. President:

Ronald Reagan (1981–1989)

Republican

Vice President: George H. W. Bush

41. President:

George H. W. Bush (1989–1993)

Republican

Vice President: Dan Quayle

42. President:

Bill Clinton (1993–2001)

Democratic

Vice President: Al Gore

43. President:

George W. Bush (2001–2009)

Republican

Vice President: Dick Cheney

44. President:

Barack Obama (2009–2017)

Democratic

Vice President: Joe Biden

45. President:

Donald Trump (2017–present)

Republican

His Vice President: Mike Pence

The Coronavirus Aid, Relief, And Economic Security Act (CARES Act)

President Trump is one of the greatest presidents that the United States of America has ever had. He has put up with a lot of disrespectful people in the media, which no other president has been treated this way, and a lot of other rude people who have also been blessed as he turned the other cheek and even gave them a stimulus check. He is a kind man to think of "America First" in such a tremendous medical crisis that we are now facing.

President Trump is the only president to get his name and signature on a stimulus check. This is the first time any president has had their name on a payment from the IRS. It is called the Coronavirus Stimulus Check. Most Americans received these checks by direct deposit and spent them buying everything from groceries to gas. Most tax paying Americans, earning under $75,000 a year received $1,200 each or $2,400 if filing joint and also $500 or each child. Anyone who earned over $75,000, for last year, was excluded from the stimulus check. It cost the government $2 trillion dollars to help the American people of our nation. This was part of the Coronavirus Aid, Relief, and Economic Security Act (CARES Act).

As of April 22, 2020, 177,6889 people have died from this virus pandemic. We are blessed by God that in Cleveland, Tennessee, Polk County, and Charleston, TN, that only one person has died. Experts say that we could possibly have to wear masks for at least a year or until the coronavirus vaccine is developed and deployed but I am praying that this virus is a rare occurrence like the viruses that have been in past years.

The Holy Bible says to "Pray Always" and I think that we can benefit by obeying God's word. Please pray for President Trump. He has a hard job and loves people of all races all over the world. We should all be doing that to make the whole earth a better world.

President Donald J. Trump, joined by Secretary of Health and Human Services Alex Azar, signs the congressional funding bill for coronavirus response Friday, March 6, 2020, in the Diplomatic Reception Room of the White House. (Official White House Photo by Tia Dufour

The Coronavirus Pandemic in Tennessee

Density of confirmed and presumptive cases of COVID-19 in counties of Tennessee.   1–9 cases   10–49 cases   50–99 cases   100–249   > 250 cases Data from https://www.tn.gov/health/cedep/ncov.html
Photo by
Leviavery Base map modified from: File:NRHP Tennessee Map.svg / CC0

County	Cases	Death	Recovered
Anderson	36	1	28
Bedford	251	4	178
Benton	6	1	5
Bledsoe	607	1	596
Blount	75	3	59
Bradley	81	1	62
Campbell	17	1	16
Cannon	13	0	9
Carroll	25	1	16
Carter	19	1	15

Cheatham	88	0	37
Chester	12	0	10
Claiborne	7	0	5
Clay	6	0	5
Cocke	20	0	16
Coffee	60	0	38
Crockett	13	1	9
Cumberland	88	1	59
Davidson	3,872	41	2,295
Decatur	5	0	5
DeKalb	29	0	19
Dickson	91	0	50
Dyer	44	0	35
Fayette	88	2	66
Fentress	6	0	3
Franklin	43	1	35
Gibson	58	1	46
Giles	9	0	7
Grainger	6	0	5
Greene	46	2	41
Grundy	30	1	26
Hamblen	24	2	17
Hamilton	342	13	129
Hancock	0	0	0
Hardeman	183	0	18
Hardin	9	0	6
Hawkins	31	2	28
Haywood	29	1	21
Henderson	12	0	10

Henry	17	0	13
Hickman	52	0	42
Houston	6	0	4
Humphreys	12	1	6
Jackson	11	0	7
Jefferson	26	0	21
Johnson	15	0	5
Knox	303	5	239
Lake	401	0	54
Lauderdale	44	0	19
Lawrence	21	0	17
Lewis	2	0	2
Lincoln	16	0	15
Loudon	48	0	42
Macon	81	3	36
Madison	160	2	142
Marion	31	1	23
Marshall	26	1	20
Maury	61	0	39
McMinn	123	12	80
McNairy	12	0	11
Meigs	22	0	19
Monroe	41	1	20
Montgomery	204	2	99
Moore	3	0	3
Morgan	12	0	6
Obion	17	1	13
Overton	14	0	8
Perry	13	0	11

County			
Pickett	1	0	0
Polk	12	0	11
Putnam	232	5	109
Rhea	7	0	5
Roane	8	0	7
Robertson	274	0	170
Rutherford	847	19	360
Scott	11	0	11
Sequatchie	10	0	6
Sevier	68	2	62
Shelby	3,681	85	2,330
Smith	24	1	20
Stewart	7	0	3
Sullivan	57	2	50
Sumner	737	41	355
Tipton	403	2	91
Trousdale	1,382	4	111
Unicoi	3	0	2
Union	4	0	3
Van Buren	3	0	2
Warren	15	0	10
Washington	66	0	59
Wayne	63	0	4
Weakley	24	0	23
White	18	0	10
Williamson	471	10	327
Wilson	318	8	195

Updated May 16, 2020

Data is publicly reported by Tennessee Department of Health

A Nashville based health care company is predicting that the coronavirus situation will get worse soon in Tennessee. By winter, we could be experiencing food shortages and weather problems along with the coronavirus situation making people extremely sick. Without proper nutrition people could die by the thousands right here in Tennessee. In Matthew Chapter 24:20, it says,

"But pray ye that your flight be not in the winter, neither on the sabbath day: For then shall be great tribulation, such as was not since the beginning of the world to this time, no, nor ever shall be. And except those days should be shortened, there should no flesh be saved: but for the elect's sake those days shall be shortened." Matthew 24-20-22 Holy Bible (KJV).

Some Things About All
50 States In America

When Is The United States of America Going Back To Work, School, Church, National Park Openings, and All Local Businesses opening?

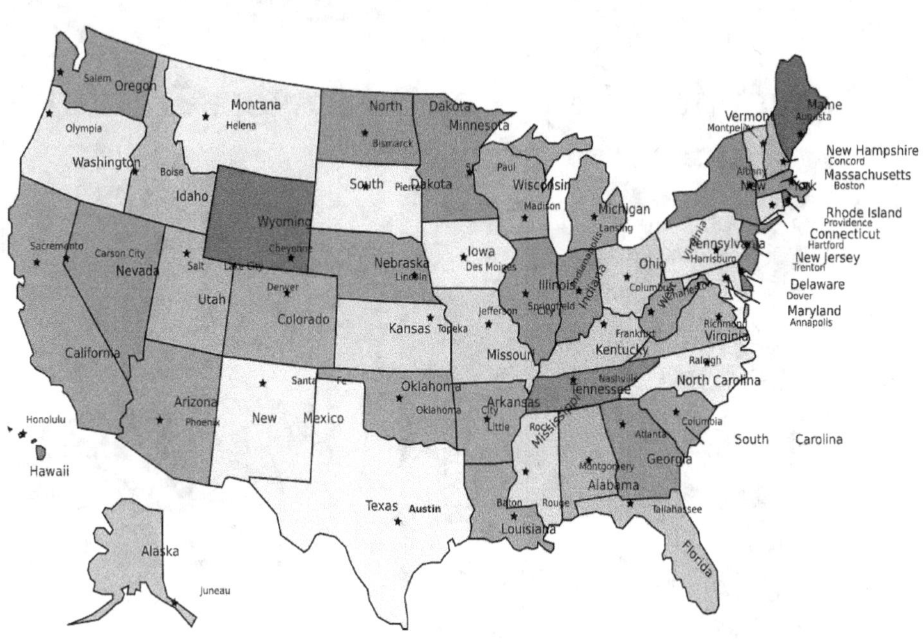

IT'S UP TO THE GOVERNOR
OF EACH STATE

Alabama

Governor: Kay Ivey　　Flower: Camellia

Photo by

Alaska

Governor: Mike Dunleavy
Flower:
Forget-Me-Not

Photo by
Alaska Governor's Office / CC BY-SA
Alaska Governor's Office / CC BY-SA
(https://creativecommons.org/licenses/by-sa/4.0)

Arizona

Governor: Doug Ducey

Flower:Saguaro Cactus Blossom

Arkansas

Governor: Asa Hutchinson

Flower: Apple Blossom

Photo by: Shane T. McCoy / US Marshals Office of Public Affairs from Washington DC / CC BY (https://creativecommons.org/licenses/by/2.0)

California

Governor:

Gavin Newsom

Photo by

Gage Skidmore / CC BY-SA

Gage Skidmore / CC BY-SA
(https://creativecommons.org/licenses/
by-sa/3.0)

Flower:

California poppy

Colorado

Governor:
Jared Polis

Photo by
US House Office of Photography

Flower:
Rocky Mountain columbine

Connecticut

Governor:
Ned Lamont

Flower:
Mountain Laurel

Photo by

Delaware

Photo by
Darwinek / CC BY-SA (https://creativecommons.org/licenses/
by-sa/3.0)

Governor:

John Carney

Flower:

Peach Blossom

Photo by
United States Congress

Florida

Governor:
Ron DeSantis

Flower:
Orange Blossom

Photo by
State of Florida

Georgia

Governor:
Brian Kemp

Flower:
Cherokee Rose

Photo by
Office of U.S. Senator David Perdue

Hawaii

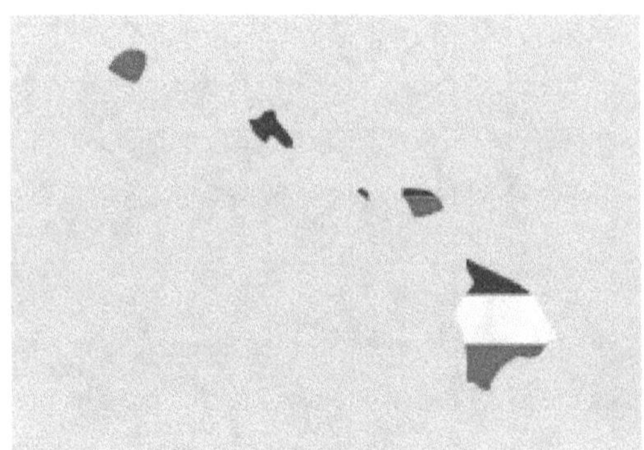

Governor:
David Ige

Flower:
Hawaiian hibiscus

Photo by
Dallas Nagata White / CC BY-SA
(https://creativecommons.org/
licenses/by-sa/4.0)

Idaho

Governor:
Brad Little

Flower:
Syringa

Illinois

Governor:
J. B. Pritzker

Photo by
Lt. Col. Bradford Leighton

Flower:
Violet

Indiana

Governor:
Eric Holcomb

Photo by
Governor Eric Holcomb / CC0

Flower:
Peony

Iowa

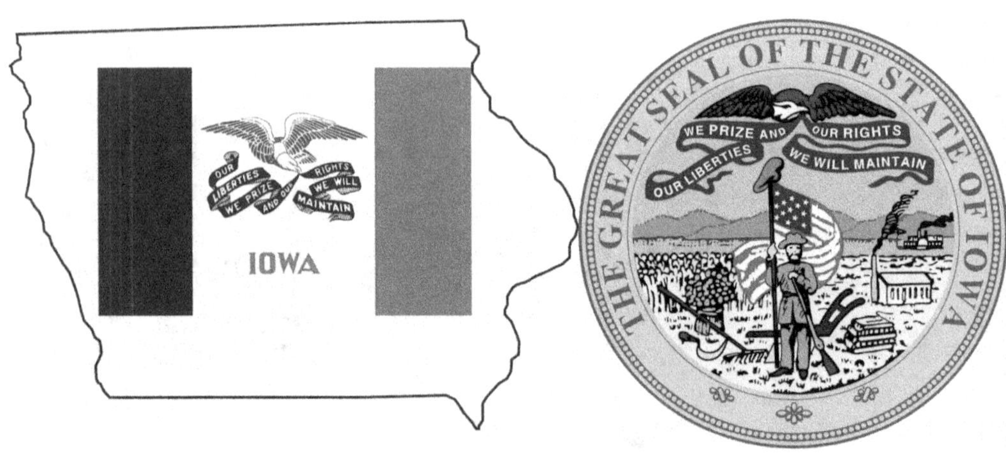

Governor:
Kim Reynolds

Photo by
Gage Skidmore / CC BY-SA
(https://creativecommons.org/
licenses/by-sa/3.0)

Flower:
Wild Prairie Rose

Kansas

Governor:
Laura Kelly

Flower:
Sunflower

Photo by
Office of the Governor of Kansas
/ CC BY-SA (https://creativecommons.org
/licenses/by-sa/4.0)

Kentucky

Governor:
Andy Beshear

Flower:
Goldenrod

Photo by
Mountain Top News / CC
(https://creativecommons.org
/licenses/by/3.0)

Louisiana

Governor:
John Bel Edwards

Flower:
Magnolia

Photo by
Richard David Ramsey / CC BY-SA

(https://creativecommons.org/licenses/by-sa/4.0)

Maine

Darwinek / CC BY-SA
(https://creativecommons.org/licenses/by-sa/3.0)

Governor:
Janet Mills

Flower:
White Pine Cone

Photo by
Rebecca Hammel/U.S. House Office
of Photography

Maryland

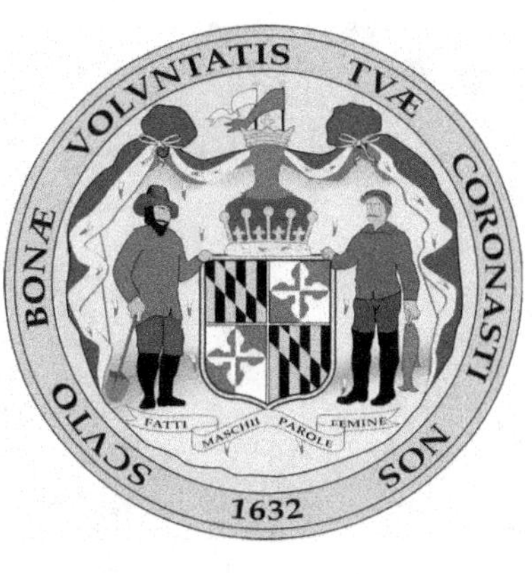

Governor:
Larry Hogan

Flower:
Black-Eyed Susan

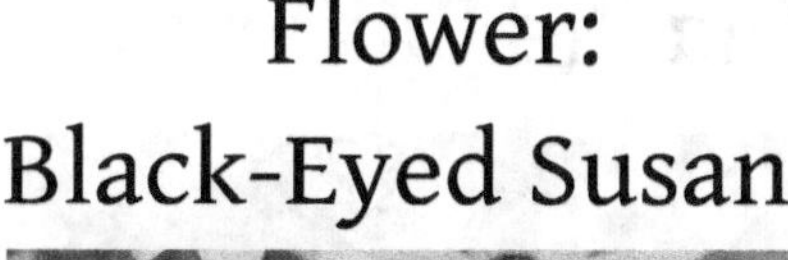

Photo by
Maryland GovPics / CC
(https://creativecommons.org/licenses/by/2.0)

Massachusetts

Governor:
Charlie Baker

Flower:
Mayflower

Photo by
Office of the Governor of
Massachusetts

Michigan

Governor:
Gretchen Whitmer

Photo by
Julia Pickett / CC BY-SA
(https://creativecommons.org/
licenses/by-sa/4.0)

Flower:
Apple Blossom

Minnesota

Governor:
Tim Walz

Photo by
United States Congress

Flower:
Pink and white
lady's slipper

Mississippi

Governor:
Tate Reeves

Photo by
The White House from Washington, DC

Flower:
Magnolia

Missouri

Photo by
Darwinek / CC BY-SA

(https://creativecommons.org/licenses/by-sa/3.0)

Governor:
Mike Parson

Flower:
Hawthorn

Photo by
Office of Missouri Governor / CC BY-SA
(https://creativecommons.org/licenses/
by-sa/2.0)

Montana

Governor:
Steve Bullock

Flower:
Bitterroot

Photo by
Gage Skidmore / CC BY-SA
(https://creativecommons.org/licenses/
by-sa/3.0)

Nebraska

Governor:
Pete Ricketts

Flower:
Goldenrod

Photo by
Gage Skidmore / CC BY-SA
(https://creativecommons.org/licenses/by-sa/3.0)

Nevada

Governor: Flower:
Steve Sisolak   Sagebrush

New Hampshire

Governor:
Chris Sununu

Photo by
Csununu / CC BY-SA
(https://creativecommons.org/
licenses/by-sa/4.0)

Flower:
Purple Lilac

New Jersey

Governor:
Phil Murphy

Photo by
Phil Murphy / CC
(https://creativecommons.org/
licenses/by/2.0)

Flower:
Violet

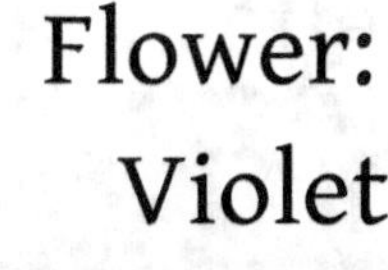

New Mexico

Governor:
Michelle Lujan Grisham

Photo by
United States Congress

Flower:
Yucca

New York

Governor:
Andrew Cuomo

Flower:
Rose

Photo of
Andrew Cuomo by Pat Arnow.jpeg: Pat
Arnowderivative work: UpstateNYer / CC BY-SA
(https://creativecommons.org/licenses/by-sa/2.0)

North Carolina

Governor:
Roy Cooper

Flower:
Flowering Dogwood

Photo by
Chris Seward / CC BY-SA
(https://creativecommons.org/
licenses/by-sa/4.0)

North Dakota

Governor:
Doug Burgum

Flower:
Wild Prairie Rose

Photo by
Office of the Governor, State of North Dakota /
CC BY-SA (https://creativecommons.org/licenses/by-sa/4.0)

Ohio

Governor:
Mike Dewine

Photo by

Vivien McClain Photography / CC BY-SA

(https://creativecommons.org/licenses/by-sa/4.0)

Flower:
Scarlet Carnation

Oklahoma

Governor:
Kevin Stitt

Photo by
Kelly White

Flower:
Mistletoe

Oregon

Governor:
Kate Brown

Photo by

Oregon National Guard from Salem, Oregon, United States

Flower:
Oregon Grape

Pennsylvania

Governor:

Tom Wolf

Flower:

Mountain Laurel

Rhode Island

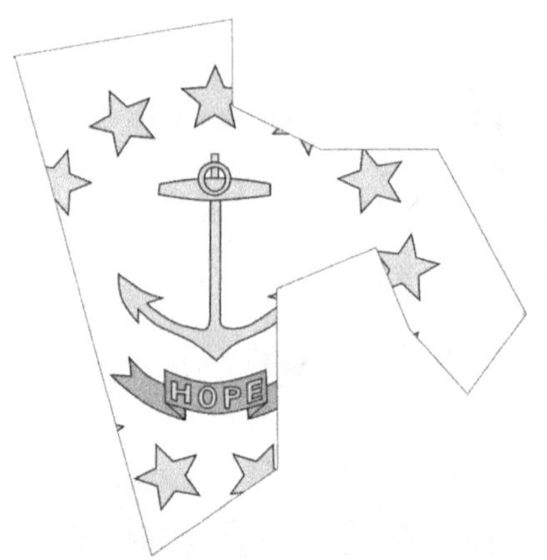

Governor:
Gina Raimondo

Flower:
Violet

Photo by
Kenneth C. Zirkel / CC BY-SA
(https://creativecommons.org/
licenses/by-sa/3.0)

South Carolina

Governor:
Henry McMaster

Flower:
Yellow Jessamine

Photo by
Staff Sgt. Jerry Boffen, U.S. Army National Guard

South Dakota

Flag from
self / CC BY-SA
(https://creativecommons.org/licenses/by-sa/3.0)

Governor:
Kristi Noem

Photo by
United States Congress

Flower:
Pasque Flower

Tennessee

Governor:
Bill Lee

Flower:
Iris

Photo by
Maryland GovPics / CC BY

Texas

Governor:
Greg Abbott

Flower:
Texas Bluebonnet

Photo by
J Dimas / CC BY
(https://creativecommons.org/licenses/by/2.0)

Utah

Governor:
Gary Herbert

Flower:
Sego Lily

Photo by
32ATPs / CC BY-SA

Vermont

Governor:
Phil Scott

Photo by
US Embassy Canada

Flower:
Red Clover

Virginia

Governor:
Ralph Northam

Flower:
Flowering Dogwood

Washington

Governor:
Jay Inslee

Flower:
Coast Rhododendron

Photo by
Office of the Governor of the State
of Washington

West Virginia

Photo by
Darwinek / CC BY-SA
(https://creativecommons.org/licenses/by-sa/3.0)

Governor:
Jim Justice

Flower:
Rhododendron

Elected as a
Democrat
but switched to
Republican
after six months
into his term

Photo by
Governor Jim Justice

Wisconsin

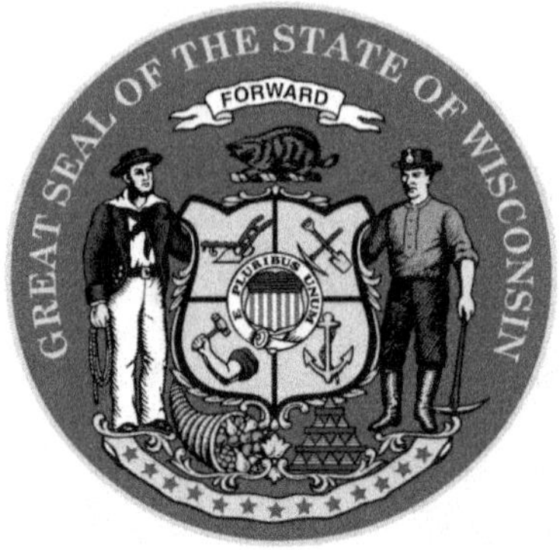

Governor:
Tony Evers

Flower:
Violet

Photo by
https://www.flickr.com/photos/
162119136@N06/42405455352/in/
dateposted/ / CC BY-SA

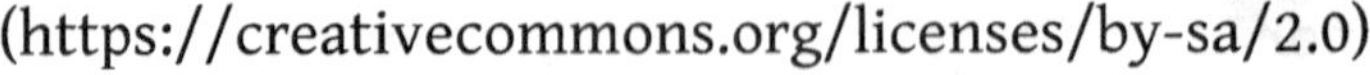

(https://creativecommons.org/licenses/by-sa/2.0)

Wyoming

Governor:
Mark Gordon

Flower:
Indian Paintbrush

Photo by
MikesGroover / CC BY-SA
(https://creativecommons.org/licenses/by-
sa/4.0)

The Flags of
The United States of America

Photo by

SiBr4 and respective authors of base files / CC BY-SA
(https://creativecommons.org/licenses/by-sa/3.0)

We Would All Love To Live
In Peace All Over The World

America and President Trump loves everyone. We should all love and respect each other all over the world. God loved all of us and sent Jesus to die for our sins so that we could go to heaven to be with Him.

Some day there will be a .... "New Jerusalem coming down out of heaven". Holy Bible, Revelation 21:2 (KJV). I want to see that, don't you?

We should all pray for each other and be prepared when Jesus comes back to get us. So, read your Holy Bible, trust God! And believe in Jesus Christ, The Son Of God, because He is coming to get His people some day.

Israel

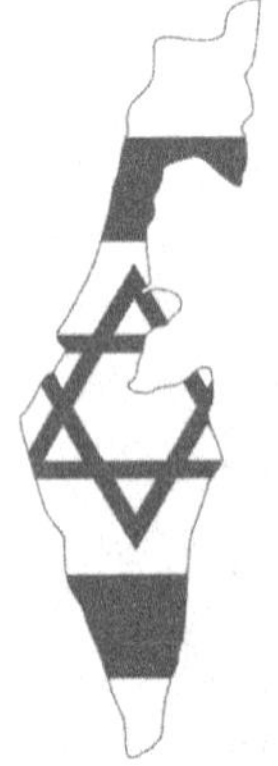  

The Prime Minister of Israel: Benjamin Netanyahu

The Flag of the Prime Minister of Israel:

Photo by
Meronim / CC BY-SA
(https://creativecommons.org/licenses/by-sa/3.0)

Israel's Capital: Jerusalem

Netanyahu meets with President Donald Trump in Jerusalem, May 2017. In December of the same year, Trump announced the U.S.A. recognized Jerusalem as the capital of Israel. He ordered the relocation of the U.S. Embassy in Israel from Tel Aviv to Jerusalem. Netanyahu agreed with his decision.

North Korea

Supreme Leader of North Korea: Kim Jong-un

North Korea's Capital: Pyongyang

Russia

President of Russia:
Vladimir Putin

Photo by
Kremlin.ru / CC BY
(https://creativecommons.org/licenses/by/4.0)

Russia's Capital: Moscow

We want a peaceful
World

"The Lord is my shepherd;
I shall not want. He maketh me to lie down in green pastures: he leadeth me beside the still waters. He restoreth my soul: he leadeth me in the paths of righteousness for his name's sake. Yea, though I walk through the valley of the shadow of death, I will fear no evil: for thou art with me; thy rod and thy staff they comfort me. Thou preparest a table before me in the presence of mine enemies: thou anointest my head with oil; my cup runneth over. Surely goodness and mercy shall follow me all the days of my life: and I will dwell in
the house of the Lord for ever."
Psalm 23 King James Version (KJV)

"For God so loved the world, that he gave his only begotten Son, that whosoever believeth in him should not perish, but have everlasting life. For God sent not his Son into the world to condemn the world; but that the world through him might be saved."
John 3:16-17 King James Version (KJV)

Index

1. The Accomplishments of Donald Trump, provided by Liberty Councel, www.lc.org

Mathew D. Staver, Esq., B.C.S.*

Founder and Chairman

Liberty Counsel

PO Box 540774

Orlando, FL 32854

(407) 875-1776 phone

(407) 875-0770 fax

LC.org

Offices in DC, FL, and VA

*Licensed in Florida and the District of Columbia – Florida Bar Board Certified in Appellate Practice

2. Donald Trump's Photos uploaded from www.wikipedia.org, www.whitehouse.gov, and www.pixabay.com

3. All scripture quotations from The Holy King James Bible

4. www.irs.gov. The Economic Stimulus Check

5. All Presidential Photos from www.wikipedia.org

www.ingramcontent.com/pod-product-compliance
Lightning Source LLC
Chambersburg PA
CBHW070707250726
48662CB00001B/301